Motherhouse

by Victor Lodato

A Samuel French Acting Edition

Founded 1830
New York Hollywood London Toronto

SAMUELFRENCH.COM

Copyright © 2010 by Victor Lodato

ALL RIGHTS RESERVED

CAUTION: Professionals and amateurs are hereby warned that *MOTHERHOUSE* is subject to a Licensing Fee. It is fully protected under the copyright laws of the United States of America, the British Commonwealth, including Canada, and all other countries of the Copyright Union. All rights, including professional, amateur, motion picture, recitation, lecturing, public reading, radio broadcasting, television and the rights of translation into foreign languages are strictly reserved. In its present form the play is dedicated to the reading public only.

The amateur live stage performance rights to *MOTHERHOUSE* are controlled exclusively by Samuel French, Inc., and licensing arrangements and performance licenses must be secured well in advance of presentation. PLEASE NOTE that amateur Licensing Fees are set upon application in accordance with your producing circumstances. When applying for a licensing quotation and a performance license please give us the number of performances intended, dates of production, your seating capacity and admission fee. Licensing Fees are payable one week before the opening performance of the play to Samuel French, Inc., at 45 W. 25th Street, New York, NY 10010.

Licensing Fee of the required amount must be paid whether the play is presented for charity or gain and whether or not admission is charged.

Stock licensing fees quoted upon application to Samuel French, Inc.

For all other rights than those stipulated above, apply to: Abrams Artists Agency, 275 Seventh Avenue, 26th Floor, New York, NY 10001 Att: Beth Blickers.

Particular emphasis is laid on the question of amateur or professional readings, permission and terms for which must be secured in writing from Samuel French, Inc.

Copying from this book in whole or in part is strictly forbidden by law, and the right of performance is not transferable.

Whenever the play is produced the following notice must appear on all programs, printing and advertising for the play: "Produced by special arrangement with Samuel French, Inc."

Due authorship credit must be given on all programs, printing and advertising for the play.

ISBN 978-0-573-69749-4   Printed in U.S.A.   #29192

No one shall commit or authorize any act or omission by which the copyright of, or the right to copyright, this play may be impaired.

No one shall make any changes in this play for the purpose of production.

Publication of this play does not imply availability for performance. Both amateurs and professionals considering a production are strongly advised in their own interests to apply to Samuel French, Inc., for written permission before starting rehearsals, advertising, or booking a theatre.

No part of this book may be reproduced, stored in a retrieval system, or transmitted in any form, by any means, now known or yet to be invented, including mechanical, electronic, photocopying, recording, videotaping, or otherwise, without the prior written permission of the publisher.

MUSIC USE NOTE

Licensees are solely responsible for obtaining formal written permission from copyright owners to use copyrighted music in the performance of this play and are strongly cautioned to do so. If no such permission is obtained by the licensee, then the licensee must use only original music that the licensee owns and controls. Licensees are solely responsible and liable for all music clearances and shall indemnify the copyright owners of the play and their licensing agent, Samuel French, Inc., against any costs, expenses, losses and liabilities arising from the use of music by licensees.

IMPORTANT BILLING AND CREDIT REQUIREMENTS

All producers of *MOTHERHOUSE* must give credit to the Author of the Play in all programs distributed in connection with performances of the Play, and in all instances in which the title of the Play appears for the purposes of advertising, publicizing or otherwise exploiting the Play and/or a production. The name of the Author *must* appear on a separate line on which no other name appears, immediately following the title and *must* appear in size of type not less than fifty percent of the size of the title type.

MOTHERHOUSE received a developmental reading at Manhattan Theatre Club, directed by Leah C. Gardiner, with the following cast.

MAE	Lynne Thigpen
EVELYN	Lisa Gay Hamilton
CLIVE	Dion Graham
ROSS	Kevin Jackson

MOTHERHOUSE was supported by a residency and public staged readings at the O'Neill Playwrights Conference of the Eugene O'Neill Theater Center, Waterford, Connecticut.

MOTHERHOUSE was developed through The Playwrights Foundation's Bay Area Playwrights Festival.

Mr. Lodato is a Guggenheim Fellow, as well as the recipient of the L. Arnold Weissberger Award for *MOTHERHOUSE.*

CHARACTERS

MAE – Clive and Evelyn's mother, fifties.
CLIVE – Thirties, thin.
EVELYN – Thirties.
ROSS – Friend to Clive, thirties.

All are black.

A Note on casting: *MOTHERHOUSE* was conceived for a cast of African-American actors. The author is agreeable to productions with actors of other races; but please note that the play works best if the entire cast is of the same race.

ACT I

Scene One

(Lights up on a small kitchen. MAE sits at the table, smoking a cigarette. She keeps glancing at a closed door, stage right – occasionally shaking her head. Picks at breakfast food. After a few beats, she yells.)

MAE. What are you doing in there?

CLIVE'S VOICE. What you *think* I'm doing?

(pause)

MAE. *(to herself)* I don't know what you're doing in there. *(pause; then yelling)* I don't know what you could be doing in there. In there fifteen minutes now. *(to herself)* Could be doing anything in there.

CLIVE'S VOICE. What?

MAE. I said you could be doing anything in there.

CLIVE'S VOICE. That's right, could be doing anything – but I am doing the thing you do in here.

MAE. Well, don't be talking to me while you doing that. You just do it.

CLIVE'S VOICE. You the one started talking. *(pause)* Ain't you the one started talking?

MAE. I'm not saying nothing.

(pause)

CLIVE'S VOICE. And don't pour my coffee out. I'm gonna finish that.

(MAE gets up, goes over to the closed door, leans in to listen.)

(Beat, then telephone rings, startles MAE.)

CLIVE'S VOICE. I ain't here, that's for me.

MAE. *(moving away from door toward telephone)* Do I know you ain't here? Do I know that? I know that. How many times you gonna tell me you ain't here? *(answers phone)* Hello…Oh, hey there, Loreen…Ain't you sweet. Same to you…Just done with our breakfast, just sitting…No, she still sleeping – but I got the boy over here…Yeah, he show up last night…He in the bathroom, he been in there twenty minutes…I don't know – and you can't ask him, you know, he gets all up on you…

CLIVE'S VOICE. Who you talking to?

MAE. *(still into telephone, laughing)* Ain't that the truth, girl… Still good to have him home…

CLIVE'S VOICE. Who that you got on the phone?

MAE. *(to CLIVE)* What?

CLIVE'S VOICE. Who's that on the phone?

MAE. *(into telephone)* One minute, baby, he at me with something. *(yelling to CLIVE)* I am talking to Loreen. Ain't nothing about you.

(CLIVE enters. He is filthy. Very animated.)

CLIVE. *(whispering)* What I hear you saying, he this, he that – don't even say I'm here. Shit. What I tell you?

MAE. Oh, go finish your breakfast and shut up. I'm on the phone. *(back into telephone)* God in the blue, get me to you…No, don't worry about it…No, no, we just talking…He gets going over everything…

(CLIVE slams his fist into his palm, glares at MAE.)

CLIVE. Get off the phone.

(CLIVE sits down at the table. While MAE talks, he picks at food, drums his fingers on table, stands up, then sits down again – he cannot sit still.)

MAE. *(ignoring him, into telephone)* So, how you doing?…That at you again, huh?…Mmmm, I know, I got it too…My hands, mostly…I know that pain…But I got a salve is good…No, better than that – I don't like the smell on that one...No, this a superior product. I'll get some over to you...Sure, sure, I get Clive run it over...

(**CLIVE** *bangs his fist against the table, stands.*)

CLIVE. Alright, get off the phone now. You hear me? Get off the phone.

MAE. Listen, honey, I gotta go, I call you later...Yeah, I'll get you some of it...Called HotSpot...

CLIVE. Goddammit, woman, what I say?

MAE. Listen, I call you later...Alright, baby...Same to you...Bye bye.

(**MAE** *hangs up the phone, stare off with* **CLIVE**.)

MAE. What? What you getting all up about? I didn't say nothing.

CLIVE. I get Clive run it over. I get *Clive* run it over. Are you stupid? You a stupid bitch.

MAE. Don't do that. Don't do that word in my house. You can do that word on your girls, on your trash – but you do not do that word on me. You hear me? No! You do not put that on me.

CLIVE. I am saying though – you don't understand. This is serious shit.

MAE. Because I didn't bring you up to use that word on me. Would a let you starve in your crib I know you end up with that word on me.

CLIVE. Listen to me.

MAE. Cause you gonna say you're sorry on that word – or there is nothing to talk about.

CLIVE. Mama, listen.

MAE. Are you sorry on that word?

CLIVE. Yes, yes – I'm sorry. Shit! I am sorry on that. Alright?

MAE. Otherwise, I don't care *who* is looking for you, your ass is out of my house.

CLIVE. I said I'm sorry. Goddammit. What, now you deaf? I said it. *(pause)* Alright?

(MAE shakes her head disapprovingly; pause.)

MAE. And why you didn't flush that toilet? Because don't think I don't know what you were doing in there.

CLIVE. How you know? You don't know.

MAE. In there twenty minutes!

CLIVE. Hey, what I do is my business. What – you gonna start sniffing after me? Cause that, that gonna send me right outta the house again. What a man do in the room is his business. That's a man's business.

MAE. Man's business! *(pause)* Sometimes I don't know whether you gonna make me laugh or you gonna make me cry.

(Pause; MAE continues to stare at CLIVE.)

CLIVE. Well, do something – don't just be staring at me like that. *(He moves away from MAE.)* Go and put your eyes somewhere else. *(pause)* Always on my back.

(pause)

MAE. So you gonna tell me what's going on – why you over here after we don't see you for two months?

CLIVE. Oh, now she wants to know.

MAE. Who you owe money to?

CLIVE. Not about money.

MAE. About what?

(pause)

CLIVE. Ross got took down.

MAE. Who?

CLIVE. Ross.

MAE. Shorty Ross? Letty's boy?

CLIVE. Yeah – he got took down, and he talking, he naming names.

MAE. Ross?

CLIVE. Ross, what I say? And that bitch talking.

MAE. He say about you?

CLIVE. He naming everybody, save his ass.

MAE. I can't see him doing that.

CLIVE. Well, he doing it, he doing the snitch.

MAE. He's not gonna do it on you, he know you from all the way back. And he got a loyalty to your sister – he not gonna do on you.

CLIVE. Maybe he will, maybe he won't – but anyone ask on me, you ain't seen me. Anyone come by, you don't know where the hell I am.

MAE. Come by?! Better not be coming by. I don't want nothing with that business.

CLIVE. If they do, that's all – I'm not saying they coming.

MAE. I don't know why you do this. This mess. Get in with that.

CLIVE. Don't you worry about my shit. I'm gonna get some money and then I get out of your face.

MAE. And where you gonna go?

CLIVE. Different ideas I got.

MAE. Where?

CLIVE. Places I know people. *(pause)* Cause this town just the same thing over and over again. You can't tell one day from the next. This, then that. This, then that. But never the other thing. Like they say: this, that, and the other thing. Yeah, well, where's the other thing? That's what I wanna know.

MAE. Same everywhere.

CLIVE. Yeah, well you ain't never been anywhere. I'm talking places you wouldn't even know nothing about. Out there. Outta this shit.

MAE. You stay here – that's all.

CLIVE. Something different – that's what I need. Different scenery. Where it look different. Cause this is nothing here, this is – I don't know what this is.

(pause)

MAE. What Shorty Ross got to say on you anyway? Huh? What he got on you?

CLIVE. Just get off me.

MAE. And I don't want any of that mess in my house. You better not have any of that mess on you. *(pause)* You hear me?

CLIVE. I ain't carrying no shit. *(pause)* I don't even do that shit anymore.

MAE. Look at your eyes. You think you gonna lie to me?

CLIVE. I didn't bring no shit in the house.

MAE. Don't even think about it. Your sister find out, she cut your head off. She cut that big ass head right off. *(pause)* After what went down on that one –

CLIVE. *(quietly)* Don't bring that shit up. Leave that alone.

MAE. She don't got no toleration for that business.

CLIVE. Yeah, I know, you don't have to tell me.

MAE. Just don't say nothing around her. About none a this. Shorty Ross, nothing.

CLIVE. Do I look stupid?

MAE. Matter a fact, you do. So I'm telling you: don't say nothing around her.

CLIVE. I know.

*(Pause; then **CLIVE** sits down at the table, drinks his coffee.)*

CLIVE. Now this cold. Shit!

MAE. More on the stove.

*(**MAE** gets the pot from the stove, pours more into **CLIVE**'s cup.)*

CLIVE. *(quietly)* I forgot about that.

*(**MAE** pours herself some coffee, then returns the pot to the stove.)*

MAE. This is a house, Clive – and there are things in a house. Hot on the stove. That's what you left behind. Hot on the stove.

(Beat. Then, from offstage, a woman begins to sing. Her voice is strong, empowered as it is by anger – but ringing

out of a great well of sadness. **CLIVE** *and* **MAE** *will occasionally speak over the song.)*

EVELYN'S VOICE.

Who loves his sugar, who loves his candy?
I know some boys that do.
Who's got a smile that works like a charm?
I know some boys that do.
And who's got a voice that's deep and that's warm?
Well – there's more than a few.
But, who's got my heart held in his palm?
You know there's no one but you.
No, baby, no one but you.

Now, who's done me wrong, who's broken their vows?
I know some boys that have.
Who's pushed me, who's shoved me, who's beaten me down?
Oh, I know some boys that have.
Who's taken my best, then walked out the door?
It's quicker to list who has not.
But, who's fled with my heart, and left me in sorrow?
You know there's no one but you.
No, baby, no one but you.
No one, no one – but you.

(A few moments of singing before **CLIVE** *speaks.)*

CLIVE. What she doing?

MAE. Shhh. How she starts the day.

CLIVE. Why she singing?

MAE. Shhh. Never ask why a person singing. Let them sing. Let the child sing.

(The song rises. **MAE** *and* **CLIVE** *listen. After a few beats,* **CLIVE** *speaks again.)*

CLIVE. I didn't know she could sing.

MAE. Would you shut up.

(Singing continues. Continues.)

CLIVE. How long she gonna sing for?

MAE. Shhh. Let it be. This how we do it.

(Singing continues, and, after a few more moments, ends.)

MAE. *(yelling)* He heard that, girl. He heard that one.

(CLIVE stares at MAE. The song has acted upon her like a drug: she is strangely calm, almost blissful.)

CLIVE. What up with the two of you?

MAE. *(still in her reverie, not to CLIVE)* Sad, you know, but it pretty. *(looks at CLIVE, sings)* Who's fled with my heart, and left me in sorrow? You know there's no one but you. *(then looks away from CLIVE)* How is it a sad song like that somehow make you happy? Make you think you gonna start all over again, get it all back.

CLIVE. Get what back?

MAE. *(not looking at CLIVE)* What we lost – everything – all come back.

CLIVE. What you lose?

MAE. *(not unkindly)* Just drink your coffee and shut up.

(MAE joins CLIVE at the table, drinks coffee. The song's spell is still on her.)

MAE. That's good coffee. *(pause)* Ain't that good coffee?

(CLIVE nods, a low mumble of agreement as he drinks.)

MAE. That's good, ain't it?

CLIVE. I said yes, I said it's good.

MAE. I put a little chicory in it.

CLIVE. You know, you getting weird. Both of you.

MAE. What, you don't like the taste?

CLIVE. Not the coffee. You just acting weird.

MAE. Let's just have some peace now.

CLIVE. Ain't gonna be no peace with you acting like that. Set me on edge. The way you talking, going on about the coffee.

MAE. Yeah, and what about you? Thinking somebody after you. Thinking Shorty Ross is gonna do on you.

CLIVE. Don't change the subject. This about you.

MAE. No. This about you. We living our life, me and your sister. We doing our days the way we do it. You the one traipse in here from outta the blue. Mind all twisted up.

CLIVE. What, you don't want me here? That what you saying?

MAE. What I'm saying is I got plenty troubles with that one in there *(indicating hallway)*. With your sister. And now I gotta have you out here with one of your stories.

CLIVE. I don't got no story. What I have is a number of facts. What I have is a situation.

MAE. Notions nothing to do with reality. Acting like you in some kinda movie.

CLIVE. What, you don't believe me?

MAE. Child, how many times have you come over here like this – filthy – look at you. Acting like they out to get you.

CLIVE. They are out to get me. You think I, I, I – What? – you think I'm making this shit up.

MAE. You scared, Clive – because the devil is on you.

CLIVE. Oh, here she go.

MAE. You scared. That's all. I can feel it right here. *(She touches her chest.)* I can feel it right here when you this close to me. In my own body I feel how scared you are.

CLIVE. *(gesturing wildly with his hands)* You talking shit. Because this is not about being scared. This about bad things coming down!

MAE. What's coming down?

CLIVE. *(still gesturing)* All around. You, you don't see it?

MAE. Your mind is turning things, baby. You mind is turning things around cause of the fear.

CLIVE. You don't see it?!

MAE. I see the darkness on you. I see it all over you.

(**CLIVE** *stands. Sudden shaking rage.*)

CLIVE. Shut up! Shut the fuck up! You don't know what you talking about! This is, this is real. This is the, the real world. This is out there. This is what you don't understand. This is not in the house, this is not singing. This is out there. This is the real.

MAE. Alright, baby, just, just take it slow. I'm only saying it's like how you get it sometimes turned around in your mind. Like you done before, thinking this or thinking the other thing. When there ain't nothing.

(**CLIVE**'s *movements become manic; he walks, he spins, he gestures wildly.*)

CLIVE. No, no, you don't know. You do not know. What, what's coming? You don't know. What's behind you? You don't know. This how it is out there. And you're not gonna turn your head, show that fucker behind you you're scared. You keep on walking. And then your shoulder start going. See now your shoulder start going. Start twitching. Like that. (*His movements become progressively more grotesque.*) Cause you not gonna turn your head, but you know that that that something behind you. Somebody behind you. And your shoulder just going like crazy. That is, that is the reality. And is that coffee good or not don't fucking matter.

MAE. (*standing*) Alright, alright, I see you baby. I see you.

(**MAE** *starts to move toward* **CLIVE**, *but he moves away.*)

CLIVE. Don't gimme that. What you see? You don't see me. What, what you see? Huh?

MAE. Listen to me, Clive.

CLIVE. There she go with the name again. Don't be saying my name. What I tell you? You don't know who's listening. (*whispering*) I get *Clive* run it over. I get *Clive* run it over.

(**MAE** *reaches out a hand; she attempts to speak, but* **CLIVE** *interrupts her.*)

CLIVE. Just shut up. Just shut up. Now you got me all – I'm all – *(a sudden exhaustion).* I can't listen to you. I can't listen to you just now. I, I, I gots to go to the bathroom.

(CLIVE moves toward the bathroom.)

MAE. Clive.

CLIVE. *(to himself)* Shit! Talking that shit. Shut the door on that.

(CLIVE goes into the bathroom, closes the door. MAE stares after him.)

MAE. Clive!

(Several beats; then EVELYN enters from stage left hallway. She wears a bathrobe. MAE does not see her. EVELYN regards MAE for a moment, then speaks.)

EVELYN. When did he get here?

(Pause; MAE does not turn to face EVELYN.)

EVELYN. Mama.

MAE. Last night. *(Pause; then she turns to EVELYN.)* We'll let him stay just for a couple of days.

EVELYN. I didn't hear him come in last night.

MAE. He knocked on my window. Then I let him in the door. *(pause)* He didn't want to wake you.

EVELYN. He didn't want to wake me – no. Because you know what I would have said to him?

MAE. He think he in trouble.

EVELYN. He's always in trouble.

(EVELYN sits at the table.)

MAE. He don't look too good.

(pause)

EVELYN. You gonna get me some coffee, or what?

(MAE gets EVELYN her coffee.)

MAE. He like your song. He heard that. He said he didn't know you could sing. He said how happy he is to hear you going with that song.

EVELYN. Look at you. Soon as he walks in the door, you on with the lies.

MAE. No, no – he said that.

(*EVELYN gives MAE a stern look.*)

MAE. Well, he say something like that.

(*pause*)

EVELYN. Why do you let him in?! That's the thing I don't understand. Why you gotta go and let him in?

MAE. Not gonna turn my children away. And this ain't to do with you anyway.

EVELYN. Don't you tell me this ain't to do with me. You think him coming in here dragging that trouble after his ass – you don't think that got to do with me? After what they done on me.

MAE. Let's not start on that.

EVELYN. This is not his house anymore.

MAE. Always gonna be his house.

EVELYN. After what they done on me – no, this is not his house.

MAE. He didn't have nothing to do with that. You can't blame him for that.

EVELYN. I blame every man. Every man in with that shit.

MAE. He didn't bring any of that mess in the house – I already ask him.

EVELYN. And you gonna believe him?

MAE. We let him stay just for a couple of days. That's all. Let's just get us through that.

(*pause*)

EVELYN. You think there's real trouble coming down on him?

MAE. He say so, but I think he's doing it up in his head. The way he talks like he got something biting his ass.

EVELYN. And we gotta listen to that!

(*EVELYN stands, gets milk for her coffee from refrigerator.*)

EVELYN. And today is my day. *(pause)* Mama.

MAE. I know what today is.

EVELYN. I'm gonna leave in a little while…for my…to do my business – and I don't want him in the house when I get back.

MAE. Maybe you just stay home today. Don't bother with that other stuff.

EVELYN. Don't get on me with that. I am going. Don't even try.

MAE. Because you can't keep doing this, Evelyn.

EVELYN. Did you hear what I said?

MAE. Alright – I'll tell him to go out for a bit.

EVELYN. Because that's our business.

MAE. I'll make him go out for a bit.

EVELYN. Because we need our privacy. I need to have my time. You know that. Today is my day.

MAE. Alright. You come home, and we do it the way we always do it. I get him out of the house – so stop on that.

(pause)

EVELYN. I bet he doesn't even know what day is today.

MAE. I'm sure he don't.

(pause)

EVELYN. *(softly)* Today is my day.

MAE. Evelyn, look at me. Look at me. Gonna be your day just the same. You go get dressed.

*(Pause; **EVELYN** and **MAE** regard one another.)*

MAE. Alright?

*(**EVELYN** nods but does not move. Pause.)*

*(**CLIVE** bursts out of the bathroom, energetic. He sees **EVELYN**, hesitates – then speaks.)*

CLIVE. Hey there, Evie. How you doing?

*(Pause; **EVELYN** does not respond.)*

CLIVE. Look at you. You looking good. *(pause)* What you do to your hair? What that on the side? You got some kinda color in it?

MAE. What you going on about? That her hair, she got gray in her hair.

CLIVE. Gray?! How she get gray in her hair? Gray? That like the bride of Frankenstein. But, I mean – no, you look good. That look good on you, Evie. That make you, you know, distinctive – they say *distinctive* when you got some gray in your hair. Dignified like.

MAE. Shut up going on about that. *(pause)* I told her to put some dye on that, but she don't want to do it. Shouldn't even have any gray at her age. I didn't get my gray till I was fifty. Now they all getting gray, they still children. The boy bring the paper, he got gray hair. *(pause)* You know, Evelyn, you really should put a little dye on that.

EVELYN. Both of you shut up. Get off my hair.

CLIVE. Make me think: could it be that long? That's what I'm saying. Cause I don't remember it being like that last time I saw you. When was the last time? Could it be that long ago? Cause that gray got me going now. That tripping me out.

EVELYN. My hair is tripping you out, huh? That the thing got you going, huh? My hair?

CLIVE. That's what I'm saying. *(pause)* When was the last time I see you, Evie?

EVELYN. I don't recall, Clive. Been a while.

CLIVE. You never here when I stop by.

MAE. Stop by?! When you stop by? Don't that make it sound nice? Is that what you're doing now, Clive: stopping by? If you are, then sit down and shut up.

(Pause; then **CLIVE** *sits at the table.)*

CLIVE. Just seem she never here when I – you know, when I get the time to come by.

EVELYN. I work, Clive – this thing called a job. And if I *am* here when you show up – I just usually don't come out of my room.

(Pause; **CLIVE** *and* **EVELYN** *regard each other for a moment.)*

CLIVE. Well, then get in there. If that's how you gonna do it.

MAE. Come on, now. Can't we just do a little kindness?

CLIVE. No, not if she can't – cause I was trying for that. I was trying for a little kindness.

EVELYN. *(to* **MAE***)* Two days at the most. Two days at the most is he welcome here.

MAE. Go on and get dressed.

CLIVE. *(to* **EVELYN***)* I get me some money, I be out tomorrow. I be on my way.

EVELYN. How much you need get you out today?

MAE. Enough, now. You go get dressed, Evelyn. I laid your dress out on my bed.

*(***EVELYN*** walks toward hallway, stage left.)*

CLIVE. And, hey there, Evie…

*(***EVELYN*** stops, her back to* **CLIVE***.)*

EVELYN. What?

CLIVE. I would appreciate it if you don't tell nobody I'm here.

EVELYN. You are not here, Clive. That's where you're mistaken. You're not here. You may think you're here. But you somewhere else.

*(***EVELYN*** exits. Pause.)*

CLIVE. What she mean by that? Where am I?

MAE. Don't ask me. I don't know where you are.

CLIVE. Am I sitting here? *(starts to wave his hands in front of* **MAE***'s face)* Am I? Am I not a thing you see in front of you? Look at that. See how I'm doing that? You see that?

MAE. *(slapping his hands)* Stop doing that.

CLIVE. See that: you see me.

MAE. I see a little part of you maybe is all.

CLIVE. I am *all* here. This is *all* there is.

(pause)

MAE. *(slowly, calmly)* Let me ask you a question.

(pause)

CLIVE. *(impatient)* Ask me. Why you talking so slow?! Ask me. What do you wanna know?

MAE. *(still slowly, not rising to* **CLIVE***'s mania)* Do you know what day it is today?

CLIVE. *(self-satisfied)* As a matter of fact, I do: it's Sunday. See, you think I don't know what day it is, and I know what day it is. My mind is on the spot. I know what day it is: so don't be trying to make me out like I'm not on the spot.

MAE. What I am asking you is do you know *what* Sunday it is: what *particular* Sunday it is.

CLIVE. You asking the number? I don't know the number. A man don't need to know the particular number.

MAE. Not the number, Clive. The day. You see, it's a day to remember. *(pause)* Mother's Day, Clive. That set something off in your mind?

CLIVE. Mother's Day?! That not like a real day. That some made up shit. Mother's Day. You see, that day invented by the corporate complexion. That is not even a real holiday.

MAE. Clive –

CLIVE. *(plowing on)* Try to get you buy some stupid card, some half-dead flowers. Now that I think about that, yeah it coming back to me now, I did see a man in the street last night, with a bucket, got his bucket of, you know how they try to sell you the one rose. I wouldn't even buy one of those sorry looking things. *(pause)* You gonna be all mad at me now I didn't buy you one?

MAE. Clive, I don't care you buy me a rose.

CLIVE. Cause I am telling you, you ain't never seen a sadder bucket of flowers than what this man was pushing.

MAE. Can you just do it down a notch or two? Just do it down, and listen to me. I don't care nothing about your sentiments to me. I am well over that. *(whispering)* This about Evelyn.

CLIVE. What about her?

MAE. *(quietly)* Mother's Day, Clive. This the day. This the day that Jame James – this the day her boy…

CLIVE. Shit!

(**CLIVE** *stands, distraught. Pause.*)

MAE. This the day her boy –

CLIVE. I know, I know. Shit! I hate having to remember that. That's why it goes out of my mind. It goes out of my mind. *(pause)* Don't it go out of your mind, sometimes?

MAE. No. *(pause)* It don't ever go out of my mind.

CLIVE. Cause that was a long time ago now. Wasn't that a long time ago?

MAE. Three years ago today.

(pause)

CLIVE. *(genuinely concerned)* So, what – am I supposed to say something to her?

MAE. Don't seem it could be three years.

(**CLIVE** *walks toward the upstage window, which looks out onto the yard.*)

CLIVE. Like what? Say I'm sorry, say – what? What a person supposed to say?

MAE. I don't think she care you say anything to her or not. You just stay out of her way.

CLIVE. Better to forget all about that anyway. A person live, he wanna move forward.

MAE. Like you do, huh? You moving forward. You ain't thought back on it.

CLIVE. I was living here when it happened. That's enough. Don't need to go thinking back on it.

MAE. Well, she can't help herself – she gonna go thinking back on it her whole life.

(pause)

MAE. And you here with your mess. And you know she go blaming that mess. *(pause)* Of all days, you gotta come today.

CLIVE. I'd a known it was that day, I'd a stayed away. *(pause; then quietly)* Cause that is – shit! – I don't wanna be thinking about that. I mean cause that just stops you. What a person supposed to do with that information?

MAE. Nothing you can do. But since you here, at least you see what I got to deal with. *(pause)* Maybe it a good thing you here. See what that girl coming to.

(pause)

CLIVE. I could say to her like how I remember that time Jame James burn his finger on the stove, and I put that cream on it for him. You remember that? How I put that cream on and how he stop crying.

MAE. Just – just don't say nothing to her. You got to watch what you say around that one.

CLIVE. Where she getting ready to go? She going to the cemetery? I hate that cemetery, I always get hungry I go there, because you got the Hamburger Hole down the street, and you smell it from there, you get hungry, and then it hit you where you are, and then you feel sick. You know? You can't be hungry in a cemetery. That ain't right. Getting all hungry in the middle of that shit. Make you sick. *(pause)* You get hungry when you go there?

MAE. No, Clive, I do not. *(pause)* Your mind just go like a, like a whirligig, don't it?

CLIVE. So, so, is that where she going? She going to the cemetery?

MAE. She go to the cemetery every Sunday. *(checks to make sure* **EVELYN** *is not in the hallway)* But today she do the whole thing. She do it every Mother's Day.

CLIVE. Why you whispering?

MAE. Shhh. I don't want her to hear me telling you. But she do the whole thing today. Go through the whole business.

CLIVE. What? What she do?

MAE. She go get the pancakes and everything.

CLIVE. What are you talking about?

MAE. The pancakes. She do the pancake breakfast first. Like they had at the church the day Jame James got shot. That day, you remember, she walking home from that Mother's Day breakfast – that when it happened. Every year now, she go back.

CLIVE. Why she do that?

MAE. I don't know. She just gotta do it, she say. She always buy a ticket. She go. Sit by herself. Eat her pancakes. Nobody know what to say to her.

CLIVE. But why she do that?

MAE. She think – I don't know – she think somehow if she take it around again, she gonna figure something out. Like she gonna find him again.

CLIVE. You let her go by herself? You don't go with her?

MAE. I'm not gonna go with her. Sit at the church hall, everybody staring at me. And everybody know about it. All the mothers there with their kids, and she sitting there all by herself. But she don't care. She in her own mind. *(pause)* I think she losing it.

CLIVE. Tell her not to go. Why don't you just talk her out of that?

MAE. And then she wear that dress. Same dress she wearing that day. And don't matter how many times you wash it, still got the stains on it. Little dark spots from the blood. From the boy's blood.

CLIVE. *(turning away from* **MAE**) This is – I, I can't think on this. Cause I got my own shit I got to deal with.

MAE. *(pursuing* **CLIVE***)* And she walk across town in that dress. First she go to the cemetery, then she go get her pancakes, and then she walk home. She go right past the spot. Everybody looking at her like that. All these years now she doing it, I bet people just waiting to see her, hanging outta their windows, waiting for her to walk by in that dress. Kids following behind her, she say – and they laughing.

CLIVE. Jesus, Mama – why you telling me this?

MAE. It's an embarrassment to me. I get so ashamed I don't want to show my face around town. I feel sad on her and all, but I don't know: do you think she need help?

CLIVE. You asking me? I don't know, Mama. I need help. I am in deep with my own shit.

*(***CLIVE*** moves away from* **MAE***, looks out upstage window.)*

MAE. I told her I would make sure you outta the house when she get home from her walk. *(coming up close behind* **CLIVE***, speaking quietly)* But I want you here when she get home. You stay in the back, I'll tell her you out – but I want you to see how she is. Listen in on how she talk. Because I can't be alone on this anymore. Clive. *(trying to get him to turn around)* She scare me, Clive.

CLIVE. *(gesturing with his hand behind his head)* Stop breathing down my neck. Stop it.

*(***MAE*** moves away from* **CLIVE***, begins to clear the table.)*

MAE. Because I can't be alone on this anymore.

(long pause)

CLIVE. *(looking out window, quietly)* That a mess out there. Everything growing all over the place.

MAE. I can't tend to that no more.

CLIVE. You don't keep your garden?

MAE. I let that go.

CLIVE. *(still looking out window)* Look at that! Oh, my god. Look at him!

MAE. What?

CLIVE. Rat. Come out from under the shed.

MAE. *(casually)* They all around.

CLIVE. Oh, and he a big one. Look at him. He looking right at me.

(**EVELYN** *enters from the hallway, looks at* **CLIVE**. *She wears a white dress.*)

CLIVE. I hate the tails on them.

MAE. *(to* **EVELYN** *)* Don't you look fine?

CLIVE. *(still looking out window, does not see* **EVELYN** *)* Nerve on him. Looking right at me. Think he owns the place. *(knocks on the glass)* Get out! Get outta there! *(pause)* There he go. There he go now. Up the hill. Yeah, you better run, cause I could shoot you, you look at me like that.

MAE. Clive. *(pause)* Clive!

(**CLIVE** *turns, sees* **EVELYN**, *who is still looking at him.*)

CLIVE. Oh, hey there, Evie. Look at you.

(Pause; **CLIVE** *and* **EVELYN** *continue to regard each other.)*

CLIVE. Rat in the yard. That what I was talking to. Rat looking right at me.

(A beat, then lights down.)

Scene Two

(A spot slowly up on **EVELYN**, *seated. She is wearing her white dress. When she speaks, she is not overly emotional: rather, it is as if she is pondering a philosophical complexity.)*

EVELYN. See now they never found it. That always gets to me. How they never found that bullet. Pass right through him, right through his head. How can that be? One side to the other. How can a thing be moving that fast? And so small, you know, big as – no bigger than the tip of my finger. One side to the other. *(pause)* And he didn't make no sound. Only his arm flew up, hand hit me flat on the breast. Like that. Flat on my breast. *(pause)* And then he went down. On the sidewalk. And you think, something like that happen, you think you in a dream. You do. You know, you can't take it as real. Everything stop for a minute. It seem everything stop. And it got so quiet after the shot, and it seem a long time. And I look down at him, and I think: what he doing? You know? What he doing down there? Even though I heard the shot, I didn't put it together. You hear that sound everyday. You know what it is. But you can't put that sound to your own child. You – you can't do it. And the blood: what is that? You know? What is that? And why his head look like that? For a time, seem like a long time, you try to make up some kinda story in your mind. Why his head look like that. Like there another meaning – how he look down there. That about something else. Not what it is. Like maybe he playing some kinda trick on me – somebody playing a trick on me. And you going through this in your mind. And it all seem like a long time, but then later on people tell you: no, you started screaming right after. But I know there was something in between. This in-between time. Before the knowledge. Before the truth. *(pause)* You know how they say time don't stop for no man. But sometime it do, I think. Or it slow down. Because I look down at him, and it was as if time got broken, the line of it got broken, and I had to take a long step to get across from one second to the next. *(She is progressively becoming more upset.)* And I get mad at myself sometimes, thinking: why I take that step? You know? Maybe I coulda walked over into some other idea. Walked over into some other story. You know, he trip, and that, that blood, it just, you know, his soda or something – cause he always carrying his little can. You know, why didn't I go there? Why didn't they let us go there? But, see, then you look up at everybody around you, and they all step back, and their hands up in the air, and their mouths open, and some other mother screaming – and it like they all telling you: go on, cross over, get to what it is. And then you look down again, and you see it. You see how the story go.

(Lights slowly up to reveal the kitchen. We can now see **MAE**, *standing close behind* **EVELYN**.*)*

EVELYN. And I went down to him. Down to the ground. And I put my hands on both sides of his head, and I never felt such a strength, I felt I could push the life right back into him. I felt so strong. I put all my body onto him. *(pause)* But he wouldn't take it. He wouldn't take what I was giving him.

MAE. Was nothing you could do. Baby, listen to me. Was nothing you could do.

EVELYN. Had to be something I could do. I had all this strong, this, this – something moving inside me – like some kinda spirit in me.

MAE. You just feeling him moving through you. I feel your father go through me like that when he die.

EVELYN. I kneel down at the same spot today. I put my hand where his head was – and that hand, it get so hot. Why it get so hot?

*(***MAE*** attempts to put a cool rag on ***EVELYN****'s neck.)*

MAE. Here, let me put this on you.

EVELYN. Don't. I don't want that.

MAE. Cool you down.

EVELYN. I said no.

(**EVELYN** *stands, begins to walk about the room.*)

EVELYN. I'm just talking. I just got to talk through this. Think it all through. *(pause)* Feel my hand. Feel it. It still burning.

MAE. Let me put this on you. Sit down.

EVELYN. I looked for the bullet again.

MAE. Now you gonna make me mad. Sit down.

EVELYN. Don't make no sense how it just disappeared.

MAE. And you think you gonna find it after all this time?

EVELYN. It just don't make no sense. Like maybe it still going.

MAE. What still going? *(pause)* What?

(**EVELYN** *sits down at the table.*)

EVELYN. Put that on me, Mama.

(**MAE** *puts the wet rag on the back of* **EVELYN**'s *neck. Pause.*)

EVELYN. I think sometimes that maybe the bullet is still going.

MAE. Enough on the bullet.

EVELYN. I get this picture – and I know, I know it couldn't be, but just listen to me – I get this picture like it still moving. After it went through his head, it just kept going. Like it going all around the world. Killing other babies. Every time another child shot, it the same bullet.

MAE. *(exasperated)* How it gonna be the same bullet?

EVELYN. No, I'm not saying it is the same. Only in my mind it seem that way. And then I think, if it still going, it gonna come back, and it gonna find me.

MAE. Stop on that. It's not gonna find you. Don't be scared on that nonsense.

EVELYN. I'm not scared. *(pause)* I want it to come back. I want it to find me.

MAE. That's enough now.

EVELYN. When I walk by that corner, I kneel down on the ground, and I think maybe what went through him will come all the way back around, take me down at the same place.

MAE. Stop.

EVELYN. On the same day.

MAE. Stop it!

(pause)

EVELYN. Don't look at me like that. I know it's not real. It's just what I think.

MAE. Thinking gonna make it real. Cause there plenty a bullets out here. They out there like weather – got more a that than rain. And you gonna draw one to you, thinking like that.

EVELYN. Well, then, I better keep on thinking.

(Pause; MAE shakes her head.)

MAE. Why you gotta be mean on me?

EVELYN. How is that mean on you? I said that bullet on me, not on you. On me.

MAE. I know what you said.

EVELYN. Cause I do think about that.

(pause)

MAE. You as selfish as the other one.

EVELYN. Who?

MAE. Your brother. Who you think? *(pause)* The two of you! *(pause)* Should be that I could depend on my children now. After all I done for the two of you! But, no, my children, they living in some fantasy world.

EVELYN. Don't you dare compare me to him.

MAE. Why not? I don't know where the two of you come from – where it is your minds come from. Cause we didn't think like this, my generation, we lived here on the ground – not up there in the clouds. I swear, I don't know who's worse, you or him.

EVELYN. How can you even say that? After what he done on me.

MAE. And don't keep saying that. He didn't do it.

EVELYN. His people.

MAE. Weren't even his people. Some kid shooting at another kid, and Jame James just get in the way. Clive had nothing to do with it.

EVELYN. All the same. I don't care. They all got their guns. They all shooting at everybody.

MAE. But you can't blame your brother for that. Every man out there got a gun – is that his fault? You can't blame Clive for that.

EVELYN. Who am I gonna blame?

MAE. How long we gonna have to go around on this? Cause if you don't stop, I will get a doctor in on you. You hear me? Cause you headed for a hospital.

(pause)

EVELYN. I can blame whoever I want. I can blame you.

MAE. Me?! How you gonna blame me?

(EVELYN stands.)

EVELYN. I don't know. I could figure out something.

MAE. You want me to slap you?

EVELYN. Maybe how like you didn't come with us that day. You weren't there when it happened.

MAE. I couldn't have done nothing.

EVELYN. It was just me standing next to him.

MAE. What could I have done?

EVELYN. I don't know. Sometimes it seems – I don't know.

(pause)

MAE. I would not want to have seen that. To tell you the truth, I am thankful – I thank the Lord I wasn't there. *(pause)* I am sorry you had to see that, Evelyn – cause that's just pressed into your mind now, I know.

EVELYN. Cause I think sometimes…

MAE. Enough with the thinking.

EVELYN. If you had been there.

MAE. I couldn't have saved him.

EVELYN. *(becoming distraught)* Like how we used to walk together.

(**MAE** *tries to approach* **EVELYN**, *but she moves away.*)

MAE. Sit down.

EVELYN. Remember how the three of us used to walk together? Like when we went to the store or something?

MAE. Evelyn. Don't get all upset, now. Sit down.

EVELYN. Remember you used to hold his one hand, and I had the other?

MAE. Don't do this.

EVELYN. I always held his hand with my left hand – we always did it like that – I was always on his right side, and you always walked on the other

MAE. Stop. Baby. Stop.

EVELYN. He liked to walk in between us.

MAE. Why you doing this? You wanna make us cry?

EVELYN. Remember how he like to walk in between us?

MAE. I remember.

EVELYN. That's how it should have been.

MAE. We all loved him, baby.

(**MAE** *attempts to embrace* **EVELYN**, *but once again* **EVELYN** *moves away.*)

EVELYN. You don't understand what I'm saying.

MAE. Come on, sit down.

EVELYN. No! Listen to me. *(pause)* You woulda been standing on his left side, you had come with us that day, this is what I'm saying: you woulda been standing there – and that bullet woulda hit you. It woulda hit you.

(Pause; **MAE** *freezes.)*

EVELYN. And I be wishing sometimes that what happened, that that bullet went into you, and not into him.

(Pause; **MAE** *stares at* **EVELYN.***)*

EVELYN. I can't help it, it goes through my head. Because you always stood on his left. And that's where he got hit from.

MAE. What are you saying to me?

EVELYN. *(talking very fast)* But maybe it wouldn't even have killed you. You know? Went into his head, but – now, if you think where he come up to on you, he come up to about your chest. You know, maybe it woulda just went into your arm. Maybe just into your arm.

MAE. Or maybe my stomach. Or my neck. Or, no – how 'bout let it go into my heart? How 'bout that?

EVELYN. I'm only saying – cause I could picture it that way. I mean, I woulda let it come into my own heart – but you the one always stood on that side. That was your place. That's where you should have been.

(pause)

EVELYN. *(crying)* That was your place.

(pause)

MAE. *(shouting)* You hear what she saying to me? *(pause)* You hear?

*(***EVELYN*** sits down at the table.)*

EVELYN. *(lost in her reverie)* I can see you fall and everything.

MAE. *(shouting)* You hear that?

EVELYN. Why you yelling? Stop it.

*(***CLIVE*** appears in the hallway entrance. Obviously stoned, he seems to be half-asleep; his eyes flutter.* **MAE** *sees him;* **EVELYN** *does not.)*

MAE. *(to* **CLIVE***)* You hear her? This a sickness. A sickness.

EVELYN. *(her back to* **CLIVE**, *still not seeing him)* Mama. Look at me.

MAE. *(to* **CLIVE***)* You see how she talk? You see how she treat me?

CLIVE. *(as if it is difficult for him to speak)* I'm gonna have to go out for a little while.

(**EVELYN** *turns her head, suddenly alert, stands. She faces* **CLIVE**. *Pause.*)

EVELYN. What are you doing here? *(to* **MAE***)* What the hell is he doing here?

CLIVE. Mama, could you give me twenty dollars? I could, I could use twenty dollars.

EVELYN. You knew he was back there?

MAE. Because somebody got to know, Evelyn. The way you going on. This a sickness. *(turns to* **CLIVE***)* You see how she is? *(pause; then louder as if to wake him)* Clive, you see how she is?

EVELYN. What? – you gonna get his opinion on my state of mind? Look at him.

MAE. You just don't stop, Evelyn. You never stop going around. And I cannot be alone on this with you anymore.

CLIVE. *(confused)* I'm alright. I just need to get out and, and – I, I just need to get out for a little while. You two don't got to worry about me.

MAE. *(to* **CLIVE***)* Not talking to you! I'm talking to her. What is wrong with you? *(turning back to* **EVELYN***)* I can't do this with you no more, Evelyn. Going over and over and over the same thing – and ain't nothing gonna change.

EVELYN. How could you do this, Mama? Look at him – he don't got no place here.

CLIVE. I'm alright. I was moving too fast, but now I got it slowed down.

MAE. *(to* **EVELYN***)* Sometimes, you scare me – and I don't know what to do.

EVELYN. And so you invite this one into our business? Behind my back you invite this one? So, now – what – you gonna start lying to me?

(**EVELYN** *moves toward* **MAE***;* **MAE** *moves away.*)

MAE. Clive!

CLIVE. I'll pay it back to you. Just ten, twenty dollars.

EVELYN. Cause I won't have you lying to me.

MAE. Clive, you got to help us!

EVELYN. Shut up!

> (**EVELYN** *slaps* **MAE**. *Pause. Then she goes to the table, rummages through her pocketbook.*)

MAE. *(softly, to* **CLIVE***)* You got to help us.

CLIVE. Everything gonna be alright, Mama. I got it all worked out in my mind.

> (**EVELYN** *has taken a twenty from her purse. She hands it to* **CLIVE**.)

EVELYN. Here's your money, Clive.

MAE. Don't give him that. You know what he wants that for.

CLIVE. I'll pay you back.

EVELYN. You go do your thing.

MAE. No, he gonna stay with us. Clive. Clive! What's wrong with you?

CLIVE. I know what day it is, Mama.

MAE. *(pleading)* Just stay with us.

CLIVE. *(to* **EVELYN***)* I was telling Mama how I remember that time Jame James burn his hand on the stove. And he crying and crying. And how I put that cream on it, on his hand, and how he quiet down after that. After I put that cream on.

EVELYN. Just go, Clive.

CLIVE. He got real quiet after that.

MAE. *(moving toward* **CLIVE***)* We got to all three of us sit down.

CLIVE. *(a bit harsh)* No. What I say? I got to go out for a little while.

MAE. You can't go. Leave me with this one. Clive. Come on, I make you some coffee, I make you some of that good coffee.

CLIVE. Get off me. I gotta go.

*(**CLIVE** leaves.)*

MAE. *(shouting through door)* And where you think you gonna go? You know you ain't got nowhere to go. *(to **EVELYN**, quietly)* He ain't got nowhere to go.

*(Pause. **EVELYN** moves toward **MAE**.)*

EVELYN. What you trying to do?

MAE. What? Just trying to bring it all together. Evelyn, listen to me. What are we doing – what are we doing in all of this?

EVELYN. Two of you gonna gang up on me? Huh? That what you thinking?

*(**MAE** backs away from **EVELYN**)*

MAE. Get away from me. You stay away from me.

EVELYN. He don't got no place in this.

(Pause. A standoff.)

MAE. You just stay away from me. *(pause)* I'm done with you. I am done with you.

(Lights down.)

End Act I

ACT II

Scene One

(Lights up on the kitchen. **CLIVE** *and* **ROSS** *are at the table. Both men are a bit disheveled. They are in the middle of a heated discussion.)*

ROSS. I didn't recognize anything. You know? I didn't be at my mother's house for like a year. And she done it all over. Same stuff, but she done it all around, the placement – you know what I'm saying? Messed it up.

CLIVE. Same thing here. I know. Cause that's the same thing here. Like my bed used to be against the one wall, now it on the other side of the room. And that, that confuses a person.

ROSS. It does. That's what I'm saying. I was confused. I was truly confused. You want a chair to be where you remember there a chair. And you *don't* want a chair where there should be nothing.

CLIVE. No, you don't.

ROSS. Then you can't hardly walk through the house. All these chairs in my way. Cause there a certain way I used to move through that house. And now she done messed that up. Chair in the hallway. I mean, why she got a chair in the hallway now? Who gonna sit on that? What, she can't walk from one end a the hall to the other without having to sit her ass down? I mean she old, but she ain't that old. And I keep tripping on that chair – you know, get up in the dark, go the bathroom – I, I can't keep it in my mind that it's there.

CLIVE. Cause it shouldn't be there. Go against common sense.

ROSS. And it go against the way I move. Go against my body. And then the couch, she got it broken now in two parts, like a V *(illustrates with his hands)*, like that, because that couch a sectional, it goes this way or that way, however you wanna do it. And she used to have it in one good long straight line, all the parts, all one way, the way a couch should be. Now she got it in this V. I can't even sit on that. Feel like it's closing in on you. I sit in that house, on that couch, and I get so – I don't know. *(pause)* Why can't it just be the way it used to be? Why can't she just leave it that way?

CLIVE. I know. Cause they always trying to *improve* the situation.

ROSS. But the thing is: you remember something, you want to stay with that, you don't want to improve upon that. You got the idea of the house down, the *idea* of the house. That is in you mind from way back – and she gotta go and fuck with that. Doing it around like it someplace else.

CLIVE. I know. You don't know where you are.

ROSS. Like she got no respect for how the house lives in my mind.

CLIVE. You just want the house the way you learned it.

ROSS. That's all I want. You hit it on the head. The way I learned it. *(Pause; he sighs.)* Shit. Cause coming home should be easy. Light. Smooth. Slip right in.

(pause)

CLIVE. Why you go back to your mama's anyway, why you didn't go back to René?

ROSS. Hey, you in the same place – so don't be on me with that.

CLIVE. I'm not on you – I'm just saying –

ROSS. And I ain't gonna stay there long. She don't even cook the same food. Even the food don't tell me I'm home. I can't even recognize this food she making now. I swear, you look on the plate – and sometimes you can't even tell what that is down there. Cause she always trying new things now. Everything in a sauce – and I don't go for that, because that obscures the food. It's like a mystery every time you sit down at the table. *(pause)* And I just long for the old food. You know? That food I remember. What I eat in my mind. *(pause)* Sometimes I think I'm in the wrong house.

CLIVE. Yeah, so you go back with René.

ROSS. No. After I got took down, she say not to come back. *(pause)* And that's fine with me. I was done with that one anyway.

CLIVE. Nothing wrong with that one.

ROSS. Yeah, she look good – but that girl a pig. She never clean.

CLIVE. She smell good to me.

ROSS. *(territorially)* And when you be smelling her?

CLIVE. I'm just saying she – in general, you know – got a nice smell about her.

ROSS. Yeah, well, she clean herself, that's not what I'm talking about: but she don't clean her *surroundings*. And a woman's got to keep her surroundings clean, cause when I had people over, doing a little business, I was embarrassed. *(pause)* Least my mother's house is clean.

CLIVE. That is true.

ROSS. Keeps it up. You know?

CLIVE. My mother's always got soap in the bathroom. One for the sink and one for the shower.

ROSS. See, now that is a touch that I like. Woman's touch, they call that. René, she didn't have none a that. Lucky there'd be one piece of soap between the sink and the tub. You always having to be leaning outta the shower to get it. And then that soap, you know, down to nothing – it like a toothpick. *(imitating René's voice)* I ran out, she always say. I ran out. She always running out of something: soap, toilet paper, milk, donuts.

CLIVE. Necessities.

ROSS. Necessities, exactly. Always running outta something. *(pause)* But my mother always well-stocked. She think ahead. She always got extra. *(pause)* How long you been over here at your mama's?

CLIVE. I just got here. I been here maybe two weeks.

ROSS. You gonna stay?

CLIVE. That depends I get me some money or not. *(pause)* And, on that, I did want to ask you something?

ROSS. I ain't go no money. I just got outta the box. And you think I'd give you money, I had some?

CLIVE. Not saying give me money. Just listen on me for a minute.

ROSS. Not listening on you. Give you money!

CLIVE. Did I say give me money? That is not what I said.

(**ROSS** *stands*)

ROSS. What you got to eat around here?

(**ROSS** *crosses to refrigerator.*)

CLIVE. Would you sit down? We are in the middle of a conversation.

(**ROSS** *opens the refrigerator, peers in.*)

ROSS. Nothing in here. There ain't even milk.

CLIVE. She out shopping now.

ROSS. My mother never outta milk.

CLIVE. Well, we all outta milk over here – so get your ass back down.

ROSS. Though she buy that gray milk now, I don't even think it's real milk.

(**ROSS** *looks back into the refrigerator.*)

CLIVE. Ross, what you looking at? We all outta everything.

ROSS. Shit. You know? I mean – shit!

(**ROSS** *slams shut the refrigerator.*)

ROSS. *(indicating his chest)* The hunger is right here, Clive. I feel it like a, like a – you know – like a wild animal. And he big. You know? Like a moose or something.

CLIVE. A moose?! Would you sit your ass down?

ROSS. My ass wanna be in the air right now, if that's alright with you. Wanna be moving through space right now.

(**ROSS** *starts to walk about the room, moving in a somewhat bizarre manner.*)

ROSS. Something moving in me, and I gotta move.

CLIVE. See now, you gone and stirred yourself up.

ROSS. I do that sometimes. I get a thought, and then it go out all over me.

CLIVE. Well, get a hold on it. Ross. I have things I need to discuss with you. Things I need to ask you. *(pause)* Ross.

ROSS. Ask me. I'm just stretching. Letting go. See if I can't get it outta me.

(**ROSS**'s *movements become increasingly spasmodic.*)

CLIVE. I swear everybody going out of their head. Sometimes I think I am the only one left with a sanitary mind.

ROSS. There are times my body just push me around. And then…*(He snaps his fingers, stops moving.)* it stops. Oh, look at that, it stop. See it don't always stop I ask it to.

(pause)

CLIVE. Are you with me now?

ROSS. See how I slide around.

CLIVE. Yeah, you sliding alright.

(**ROSS** *starts to move around again.*)

ROSS. I get that moving in me, and I don't know am I happy or am I sad. *(All of the following he addresses to himself, attempting to evaluate his state of mind.)* Happy. Sad. Happy. Sad. Where we going? Where are we going?

CLIVE. Ross. *(pause)* Ross. Over here.

(**ROSS** *stops moving, looks at* **CLIVE**.)

ROSS. What?

CLIVE. Would you join me at the table? Because that is the way I would prefer to conduct our business. Like, like normal men – not with you jitting around like that.

ROSS. We doing business? What we doing?

CLIVE. Sit down, and we can discuss it.

ROSS. I'm listening.

CLIVE. You gonna sit down?

ROSS. I can't accommodate that right now. If I sit down, I know I'm gonna have to stand right back up again. But tell me what you wanna tell me. Don't worry, I'm done moving. I'm done moving now. *(pause)* So – what we doing?

CLIVE. Well, I was wondering if you might have a particular item – something I might be interested in obtaining from you.

ROSS. What you in need of?

CLIVE. You remember you old gun – that first one you got?

ROSS. Which one?

CLIVE. What, you don't remember your first?

ROSS. The Wild Dog?

CLIVE. No, not the Wild Dog – the little one – the Cupcake.

ROSS. Oh, yeah. I loved that little gun. That was a sweet little thing.

CLIVE. You still got it?

(**ROSS** *sits down at the table.*)

ROSS. That was my very first. Little baby gun. That was like ten years ago.

CLIVE. Do you still got it?

ROSS. I suppose it still at my mama's house. If she didn't move that too.

CLIVE. Well, you check it out.

ROSS. What you want with that little thing? That like a kiddie gun.

CLIVE. It do the job, don't it?

ROSS. Yeah, I guess so – but that ain't a gun gonna get you no respect.

CLIVE. Would you sell it to me, you still got it?

ROSS. How much you gonna gimme for it?

CLIVE. And you know it ain't worth hardly nothing.

ROSS. Course I do have the sentimental attachment.

CLIVE. Wouldn't get twenty dollar for a pawn.

ROSS. But the sentiment, Clive. The sentiment is the issue.

CLIVE. Get off that bullshit. You didn't forget you had it, you woulda already sold it.

ROSS. Maybe now – but maybe not.

CLIVE. How much you would ask for that?

ROSS. I don't even know I still got it. Stupid bitch coulda thrown it out – cause she do things like that.

CLIVE. If you still got it – how much?

ROSS. How much you offering?

CLIVE. Don't play with me: how much?

ROSS. I don't know. I'd take maybe – oh, I don't know – I'd take a ten ten.

CLIVE. For that?! No where could you get a hundred for that.

ROSS. No – cause there kids out there, you know, they inexperienced – they wanna start with something like that – they might go for it. Some dumbass kid.

CLIVE. I give you half a that.

ROSS. Fifty dollar?

CLIVE. And that's more than it's worth.

ROSS. You got the money now?

CLIVE. You get me the gun, I get you the money. I got to have the gun first. *(pause)* So – fifty dollar – you agree on that?

ROSS. Yeah, alright. I'll do that.

CLIVE. So we go check it out – see if you still got it.

ROSS. I used to keep it in a Chivas Regal bag – you know the blue velvet? – little gold ropes. I was just so cute, keeping it in my little bag. And that in my drawer under my underwear. You know, real Hollywood like.

CLIVE. Well, let's hope it still there.

ROSS. And bring that money.

CLIVE. I'm not gonna have the money. I have to have the gun for a day first.

ROSS. And why is that?

CLIVE. Cause there another party involved. It's not for me. What you think I want with a piece a shit like that? I am selling it to somebody else.

ROSS. Who you hustling?

CLIVE. Don't you worry about it.

ROSS. Come on, tell me.

CLIVE. Somebody I know need it – and they gonna give me – get this – they gonna give me five hundred dollar for it.

ROSS. *(standing)* What? Five hundred?

CLIVE. *(laughing)* Yeah. That what I said.

ROSS. *(stammering)* Five five – what? Who is gonna – five hundred?!

CLIVE. Sit down.

ROSS. I should sell it to them myself.

CLIVE. It's my deal – and you know a sucker like this come along once in a lifetime. So you be happy with your fifty dollar.

ROSS. Who this idiot gonna give you five hundred dollars for that little gun?

CLIVE. You think I'm gonna tell you?

(**ROSS** *starts to walk about the room again.*)

ROSS. Five hundred dollars.

CLIVE. And that gonna be enough to get me outta town, get me set up somewhere else, cause I am done with this town.

(**ROSS** *opens the refrigerator, peers in again.*)

ROSS. Where you gonna go?

CLIVE. I don't know. I just can't be living with these two – you know, because they just don't stop with their shit – whining or crying or what you doing in there. You know I'm saying – just get out, get myself out – and I'm saying like *away*. *(pause)* Maybe I go to California.

(**ROSS** *is still looking into refrigerator.*)

ROSS. I'd like to go there. That is a place I'd like to go.

CLIVE. Not on fifty dollar.

ROSS. Shut the fuck up. I could get me enough to go, I wanted to.

(*Pause.* **ROSS** *still in refrigerator.*)

CLIVE. Ain't nothing in there.

ROSS. I can see that.

(**CLIVE** *stands.*)

CLIVE. Listen, I'm gonna use the room – then we go find us something to eat.

(**CLIVE** *goes into the bathroom;* **ROSS** *is still looking into the empty refrigerator as he speaks – occasionally shouting out to* **CLIVE**, *occasionally to himself.*)

ROSS. Cause I could get me enough, I wanted to. *(pause)* Maybe I will. Maybe I go with you. Cause I wouldn't mind that. California. That like the sunshine state, right? Ain't that what they call it? Cause I do like the sunshine. *(pause)* Oranges. Avocados. *(pause)* What else they got there? Get you some good seafood there. Cause that right by the water, California, ain't it? Right by the ocean. *(pause)* You ever swim in the ocean, Clive? I ain't never done that. *(pause)* Would you be scared to swim in the ocean? You see that movie *Piranha*, with all those little fish eating on people's flesh? They find the bodies floating to shore, almost down to the bone. I think that took place in California. I think it did. But they, they took care a the problem. I don't remember how they did it exactly, but I remember the fish like exploding at the end. *(pause)* I think I would like to swim in the ocean. I could enjoy that. I bet they do that salt water taffy there. *(pause)* And then a course you got Disneyland. The Magic Kingdom, they call that. I bet we could sell a lotta shit in The Magic Kingdom, Clive. Make a lotta money. Selling our stuff there. *(pause)* The sunshine state.

(MAE enters, carrying bags of groceries; she stands at the door, listening to ROSS. ROSS does not notice her.)

ROSS. I think that a good idea, Clive. Cause this here is empty. This here a wasted land. You the only one a my boys left, Clive. *(pause)* This here is hollow. *(He yells into the refrigerator.)* Hollow. And it cold, too. And I was not built for the cold. No, I wasn't.

(MAE puts her groceries down on the table with a thud; ROSS turns.)

MAE. And what were you built for, Shorty?

ROSS. Mae. Miss Mae. Miss Magic Mae. Where you come from?

MAE. What you doing in my ice box?

ROSS. I was just gonna shut that.

MAE. Might as well leave it open, got things to put away.

(MAE starts to unpack groceries.)

ROSS. Been a long time, Miss Mae.

MAE. Yes, it has.

(ROSS begins to look through bags on table.)

MAE. Shorty Ross. Look at you.

ROSS. They don't call me that no more.

MAE. Why not? It still sum you up.

ROSS. You mind if I ate some of these chips.

MAE. Help yourself.

(ROSS sits down at the table, opens bag, eats.)

ROSS. You got some milk?

MAE. Should be some in one of those bags.

(ROSS looks, finds a carton.)

ROSS. *(disappointed, whining)* This ain't the real stuff. This that gray stuff. How come you buy that, too? Shit.

(MAE takes the carton away from him.)

MAE. Didn't buy it for you.

(ROSS looks through other food on the table.)

ROSS. This ain't the right food. This just like hers. Lady food.

(MAE grabs another item from ROSS' grip.)

MAE. Where Clive at?

ROSS. Bathroom.

(Pause. MAE continues to put away groceries; ROSS still eating chips.)

MAE. I had heard you were in a bit of trouble, Shorty.

ROSS. Ross. Ross is how I go now.

MAE. Yeah, well, I had heard you had some trouble.

ROSS. No big deal. Got outta that.

MAE. I had heard it was a big deal.

ROSS. No.

MAE. Clive made it out that it was some real trouble.

ROSS. Oh, he just gets that loop in his head. You know how he gets.

MAE. Yeah, I do know. That's what I thought. *(pause)* So, there's no trouble then?

ROSS. Not today.

MAE. Well, you just keep it that way. *(pause)* How's your mother?

(ROSS makes a vague gesture, mumbles something incomprehensible as he eats.)

MAE. She good?

ROSS. I don't know how she is. She just is. Yeah, she fine, I guess.

MAE. She still got that dog, that little dog, what was her name?

ROSS. I don't know.

MAE. You know. What was her name? Peaches?

ROSS. Prissy.

MAE. She still got her?

ROSS. No. Died.

MAE. Sorry to hear that.

ROSS. Died last year. And she still don't stop talking about it. *(pause)* It had a disease a the brain.

MAE. Did it, now? That musta been hard on your mama. I know she was close to that animal.

ROSS. Yeah. And she love to tell you how it died. You get with her, and that be the first thing she be telling you.

MAE. I used to see your mama all the time. I never see her no more.

ROSS. She don't go out too much. She say she get nervous walking around. What's there to be nervous about?

MAE. Don't act like that. You know there's things a woman gonna be nervous about. Anybody gonna be nervous about.

(Pause; **ROSS** *still eating.)*

ROSS. So you wanna hear how that dog died?

MAE. Died of the brain, you said.

ROSS. Yeah, that the cause – but I'm saying the story of how it died, what she always telling everybody. See that dog always sleep with her. Down at the bottom of her bed. And one night, it crawl up to her face, and she say, get back down there, you know, she move it back down by her feet. And then in a little bit, up it come again. Up to her face. Crawl right up on her chest. And she put it back down again. You know, cause its place is down at the bottom. And then this time it don't even wait – right after she put it down, you know what it do?

MAE. Come up again.

ROSS. Come up again. Exactly. Third time. Crawl up to her face. And then when she telling the story, she say: *(mocking his mother)* Oh, I knew she be needing something from me, but I didn't know what Prissy needed, so I just give her a hug. And so she hug that ugly thing, and it die right up there by her face. *(mocking mother again)* That what that dog wanted, she say, that dog wanted to die in my arms.

MAE. Ain't that something?

ROSS. You know what I said to her: I said maybe you didn't give that dog a hug, it might still be alive today.

MAE. Terrible to say that.

(ROSS laughs; MAE takes the bag of chips away from him.)

MAE. How is it you can make fun on that?

ROSS. I wasn't done with those.

MAE. You had your fill.

(CLIVE enters from bathroom, recharged. ROSS and MAE turn to him. CLIVE puts up his hands, as one does to quiet a room, to quell applause. He prepares to speak.)

CLIVE. There are certain days a person feel good. A person feel lucky. You know, cause I was in there thinking – hello there, Mama – I was in there thinking – cause Ross had pointed out earlier the importance of the cleanlihood of a house. How it important a house be clean. Because from this a man can work, he can build himself up, he can feel a sense of respect. And the deep meaning of this had not struck me until just now I was in there. Cause the sink, the mirror, they were just, they were shining – shining like a whole army – a whole army a clean. This, this inspires a man. Because what is there to stop me? What is there to, to keep me down? You know what I'm saying? When things are shining like that. And the other thing was – as I saw this, I saw a piece a hair in the sink. A piece a hair that had invaded the scene. And this was my hair – cause you know your own hair when you see it. And then the thought I had was: I do not want to be a piece a hair in a clean sink. I want to rise above that. Cause that black hair in the white sink just ruined the whole picture. And that was very – it was – it set off a number a thoughts – but mainly the thought that I do not want to be a hair in a sink. Cause the sink is clean, and to that a man should rise. To the cleanlihood of his house. A man should rise.

(Pause. MAE and ROSS stare at CLIVE.)

ROSS. That what I was trying to say to you before.

MAE. *(to ROSS)* You know what he's talking about?

ROSS. He is talking about moving out of the emptiness.

CLIVE. *(concurring)* Moving out of the emptiness.

ROSS. The Magic Kingdom.

CLIVE. The Magic Kingdom!

MAE. *(to ROSS)* Stop eggin' him on. Get him all excited.

ROSS. I ain't doing it. He excited all by himself.

CLIVE. Everything is moving forward, Mama. Everything on track.

MAE. Come sit down, Clive. I'm gonna make us something to eat.

CLIVE. No, no, Ross and I going out. We gonna get something out there.

MAE. No, now, I got everything.

CLIVE. Don't bother with that.

MAE. *(to ROSS)* You wanna join us, Shorty?

CLIVE. No, he don't – he got things to do.

MAE. *(to ROSS)* Cause Evelyn gonna be home soon. You ain't seen her in a while.

ROSS. No, Miss Mae, I don't think so.

MAE. Gonna have a nice family dinner.

CLIVE. Mama, we got things to take care of. *(to ROSS)* You ready?

MAE. Clive, I planned this all out – this dinner. Evelyn gonna be home in a little while. Be nice for us all to sit down together.

CLIVE. Don't get on me, cause I am feeling good right now. I wanna keep with that. *(to* **ROSS***)* C'mon.

*(***ROSS** *stands.)*

MAE. I don't understand you. You just saying how nice the house is. How it clean, how it make you feel good. So, you sit down, Evelyn come home; we all have a nice supper.

ROSS. *(to* **MAE***, trying to help)* The food, though, it not gonna satisfy him – see now I understand that. Cause I saw the food that you bought. It not gonna do the job.

MAE. Shorty, just, just let off. This our business.

CLIVE. Mama, listen, you save me something. I eat it later. You save me something.

MAE. Cause I notice you and Evelyn getting along a little better. And she apologize to me. And she seem better, don't she? And you in your old room. And I thought, the three of us –

CLIVE. How 'bout we do it tomorrow? We do it tomorrow.

MAE. I bought a bottle a wine for us.

CLIVE. We gonna drink it tomorrow. Alright? Cause I am making my way now. Tomorrow we celebrate.

ROSS. Five hundred dollars to celebrate.

CLIVE. Shut up.

MAE. *(to* **ROSS***)* What five hundred dollars?

CLIVE. There are just things. Possibilities. Let me make my way. Alright? Let me make my way. Let me, let me see it through. Cause I have all my feelings in the right place. See what I'm saying? And tomorrow, we gonna have a nice dinner.

MAE. Tomorrow Sunday.

CLIVE. And when Evie get back from the cemetery, we have our dinner. Alright? We do it up.

ROSS. *(impatient)* So, let's go. I'ma fall down I'm so hungry.

MAE. *(to* **ROSS***)* I thought you'd want to see Evelyn – you ain't seen her in a long time.

CLIVE. What he want to see her for? – he don't want to see her. *(pause)* Just wait on till tomorrow, Mama.

MAE. You promising me that, Clive?

CLIVE. I am. You save that food for tomorrow.

ROSS. *(at the door)* Nice seeing you, Miss Mae.

CLIVE. *(to* **MAE***)* Tomorrow. That is marked on me.

*(***CLIVE** *and* **ROSS** *exit.)*

(pause)

*(***MAE** *sits down at the table.)*

MAE. Better be marked on you.

(lights down)

Scene Two

(Lights up. MAE, at table, drinking wine. She is a little drunk. EVELYN is looking out upstage window.)

MAE. This is pretty good. You sure you don't want a glass?

EVELYN. I'm fine.

MAE. Not too sweet. I don't like it too sweet. Let me pour you a glass. I'm gonna pour you a glass.

(MAE pours wine into a glass)

EVELYN. Really do need to get that cleaned out there.

(MAE brings wine over to EVELYN, hands it to her.)

MAE. What's that?

EVELYN. The yard. Look at it. Trash all over the place.

MAE. Gonna get Clive take care a that. Now that we got him around. *(looking out window)* Get him take out that swing set. That thing's just gone to rust.

(EVELYN walks over to table with her glass – does not drink. MAE still at window.)

MAE. And that sound it make. Wake me up sometimes. When it windy. *(pause)* Not the yard it was – cause that was a place we used to spend time – sit out there – summertime. I don't know why we don't live outside like we used to. Warm days, you couldn't keep us inside. Cause that was my pride and joy, that yard. *(pause)* But we get it back, we put ourselves to it. Get ridda all that junk. Cause that creaking do wake me up sometimes. *(pause)* But we gonna do it up real nice again.

EVELYN. Needs to be oiled.

MAE. *(turning)* What's that?

EVELYN. *(a little sharp)* Chains. The chains need to be oiled.

MAE. You mean the swings?

EVELYN. That's why they make that sound.

MAE. Not gonna be bothering with oil. Just take it down. Only one using those swings are the birds. I always get a laugh I see a bird on one of those swings. They don't know what the hell it is. They think it some kind a ledge. Then they get on it, and sometimes a wind come up, you know, it start blowing. And they flapping their wings trying to keep their balance. Funny to see a bird like that.

(Pause; **MAE** *finishes the wine in her glass.)*

MAE. Mmmm – that just has a nice taste to it. The bottle say supposed to have like a cherry taste. I don't taste that – but I do like it. That a California wine.

EVELYN. I suppose you want a little more.

MAE. I'll take a splash.

*(***MAE** *goes over to table;* **EVELYN** *pours out wine.)*

MAE. Wine look pretty in these glasses. *(pause)* You ain't drinking yours?

EVELYN. I took a sip.

MAE. We ain't done this in a while. Had ourselves a bottle a wine.

(pause)

EVELYN. When Clive say he's coming back?

MAE. He say he be back later – but you know him. Tomorrow, though, we gonna have supper all together. Have to remember buy us another bottle. Gonna copy down this label, get this again.

EVELYN. So Clive say he be back late?

MAE. Didn't say. *(pause)* I'm glad you two getting along better.

EVELYN. Just making do.

MAE. More than making do. You two talking on the porch the other day, look like you making amends.

EVELYN. Settling some things between us.

MAE. Good on that. Good on that.

*(***MAE** *reaches out her hand to touch* **EVELYN***'s arm.)*

MAE. Makes me happy to have my children with me.

*(***EVELYN** *gently pulls her arm away from* **MAE**.*)*

EVELYN. I wouldn't know about that.

MAE. Don't sour this. This a nice evening. C'mon gonna make a toast. Pick up your glass.

EVELYN. Ain't nothing to toast.

MAE. Pick up your glass.

EVELYN. Why?

MAE. Because I ask you. We gonna have a toast.

EVELYN. Look at you. You drunk.

MAE. Oh, I am not. Come on, sourpuss, lift that glass.

(Pause. **EVELYN** *lifts her glass. Pause.)*

EVELYN. Well?

MAE. Thinking what I wanna say. Alright, gonna toast to my children.

(pause)

EVELYN. Is that it?

MAE. To my children. And to me with my children. What? Why you making that face? That's what I wanna toast to. It's my toast. *(pause)* Now I'm gonna say it again: To my children. And to me with my children. And to our life, and what we gonna do with it. *(pause)* Alright, hit me.

(They clink glasses; **MAE** *laughs, drinks.)*

MAE. Least get your lips wet.

*(***EVELYN** *takes a small sip.)*

MAE. Now that wasn't too hard, was it?

(pause)

MAE. What's wrong with you?

EVELYN. Nothing.

MAE. Cause everything is good, Evelyn. I'm telling you, everything gonna be fine.

EVELYN. Is it?

MAE. Yes. It is.

EVELYN. I suppose wine make it look that way.

MAE. Not the wine. The truth make it look that way. The truth.

EVELYN. Why don't you go to bed?

MAE. You don't believe me?

EVELYN. Believe what?

MAE. That everything gonna be fine.

EVELYN. Alright, Mama.

MAE. I got a whole list a things – get the house back to where it was. And we all gonna do our part – you and your brother and me – and we gonna live in the house again. Like we used to. Live in the house – like a house need to be lived in. Cause this house like a ghost house.

EVELYN. I think you need to go to bed.

MAE. But that's in the past – everything gonna be better now.

EVELYN. And how exactly do you arrive at that?

MAE. I know it is – I feel it.

EVELYN. Because that is not what I get when I add things up.

MAE. You adding things up wrong is all.

EVELYN. Oh, is that what I'm doing?

MAE. Yes. You taking old things into consideration when you should be looking forward. And you gotta make yourself look forward – look at me – you gotta force yourself to do that – cause the past, it easy to stay there. I could live there I wanted to. Cause no matter how bad it is, the past is easy – the past like a warm bath – but you stay in there too long you gonna shrivel up.

EVELYN. Mama, I don't want to talk about this anymore.

MAE. Oh, now she don't want to talk. No, but when you go on it's alright, huh? Well, now I'm going on a little bit – cause I got ideas in my head too – not just you and him – I got my own ideas – and those the ideas that gonna rule this house.

EVELYN. Go to bed, Mama. Please.

MAE. I could surely live in the past, I wanted too. Just cleaning the floor could pull me back to that. You know, sometimes I be cleaning the floor – and I think I smell your father's feet – cause that man had him some loud smelling feet. Or maybe I think I smell his cigarettes – because sometimes when we arguing, he used to put out his cigarettes on the floor – you know, to make me mad. To disrespect my house. And if I am down there, all that stuff rise up outta the boards. Cause the past smell – and not sweet. And if I didn't pick myself up, I'd be down there cleaning forever – cause you never gonna get that clean.

EVELYN. Enough, Mama.

MAE. But, you see, I don't stay down there – I pick myself up. I look to the future. See now how I made that toast – because I am not afraid to ask for something. So, yes, your mother is drinking a little bit, she a little drunk – but what I am doing is drinking and wishing at the same time. Cause there are blessings yet to come. See now we used to pour a little wine on the floor, my mother did that. A little wine on the floor.

(MAE stands, pours a little wine on the floor.)

EVELYN. Stop that.

MAE. Just a little bit. A blessing on this house. Because that's come due. And we gonna take it, we gonna take everything God wanna give us. Because we deserve it. *(pause)* Look what he gave us already.

EVELYN. What did he give us?

MAE. Brought Clive home. Brought my son home.

EVELYN. He's gonna have to do better than that.

MAE. Cause I been praying that he come home.

EVELYN. Why – you want another smell to clean up after? Cause that's a real rotten one.

MAE. *(a bit unsteady on her feet)* No, don't you do that. Don't try to get between me and my son. You always doing that.

EVELYN. I don't know why you can't see him – see what he is.

MAE. I know he got his problems – but he came home, he came home to us. And how I heard him talking today, he trying to get himself together.

EVELYN. Oh, please – trying to get himself together – Mama, everything out of his mouth is a lie.

MAE. Saying how the house is clean. How he want to be clean inside the house. He was rambling like he do – but he trying to get at something, I could see that. He trying to get at something better.

EVELYN. Alright, Mama – I really think it's time for you to go to bed.

MAE. We all trying to get at something better. But not you, you always taking it back, always taking it back to where it all sad and where everything seem wrong – but I don't want to go there.

EVELYN. No, I guess you don't.

MAE. And ever since Jame James died, I think you scare off Clive with all your sadness. That what make him go even deeper into that mess. Cause he don't want a part in that sadness either. He trying to get at something better.

EVELYN. Well, maybe you should just hitch up with him then and ride on. Go ahead. See where that lead you.

MAE. Maybe I will.

EVELYN. Do it. I'm not gonna hold you back.

MAE. No, you ain't. Because he my son – and that's something you don't understand. He my son. And he gonna stay in this house. *(pause)* You hear me?

EVELYN. Well, then I'll just back out of the picture.

MAE. You do that.

EVELYN. Since you seem to have your mind made up.

MAE. I do. And you ain't interfering. Not this time.

*(**MAE** teeters, then regains her balance. Pause.)*

MAE. *(exhausted)* How'd we get here? We were just having us a nice glass a wine. How did we get here?

EVELYN. We always end up here, Mama.

MAE. Cause you don't have to be out of the picture. We could all be in the picture together.

EVELYN. We'll see how it goes.

MAE. Cause don't nobody know what the future hold – but a person can ask that it be a certain way. A person can ask for something.

   (EVELYN gets up, extends a hand to MAE.)

EVELYN. Here, come on. Get yourself into bed.

   (MAE leans on EVELYN; they begin to walk toward the hallway.)

MAE. And remember, we gonna have a nice dinner tomorrow. The three of us.

EVELYN. Sure. We gonna get it all settled.

MAE. You come to bed now, too.

EVELYN. No, I'm gonna wait up a bit.

MAE. You gonna wait for Clive?

EVELYN. I'm just not tired yet.

MAE. You wait up for Clive. Cause that your brother.

EVELYN. I know.

MAE. That your brother.

EVELYN. Good night, Mama.

MAE. And he love you.

   (MAE lets go of EVELYN just before the hallway.)

MAE. Your brother. Son. My son.

   (MAE exits. EVELYN returns to the table, sits. Beat. Then her body convulses as she begins to cry. She covers her mouth to muffle the sound.)

   (lights down)

Scene Three

(Lights up on **EVELYN**, *alone in the kitchen. She is looking out the back window. After a moment, she goes over to the table, clears the wine bottle and glasses. She pours the wine from her glass into the sink; if there is any left in the bottle, she discards this too, throws the bottle into the trash.)*

(A few more moments of **EVELYN** *alone – then* **CLIVE** *enters. He is in slow mode: stoned or drunk. He carries a blue velvet Chivas Regal sack.* **CLIVE** *and* **EVELYN** *regard each other for a moment, before dialogue begins.)*

CLIVE. *(a little too loud)* Hey there, Evie.

EVELYN. Shhh. She sleeping.

*(**CLIVE** walks over to the table. Pause.)*

CLIVE. She sleeping?

EVELYN. Yes.

CLIVE. What time is it? Ain't it early?

EVELYN. No, it's not – it's late.

CLIVE. Is it? I can't tell is it early or is it late. Lose track a time, sometimes – you know? *(pause)* She sleeping, huh?

EVELYN. Again with that. Yes.

(pause)

CLIVE. Because she a light sleeper.

EVELYN. She had herself almost a bottle a wine – she's not getting up anytime soon.

CLIVE. You got anymore a that?

EVELYN. What?

CLIVE. The wine.

EVELYN. No. All gone.

(pause)

CLIVE. Cause I could use a little wine.

EVELYN. You look like you doing fine.

CLIVE. I'm doing alright – just to take the edge off, I woulda had me some.

EVELYN. You on edge, Clive?

CLIVE. You know – to settle the mind – that's all – cause sometimes it seem a little bit off.

EVELYN. What's that?

CLIVE. Everything. Everything seem off center. Outta place. You know what I'm saying?

EVELYN. No, not really, Clive.

CLIVE. Everything. Every time I come home – get stranger and stranger around here. Like when I was walking here just now, when I was outside, coming up upon the house, I seen the light over the door, and how it shine on the number, you know the house number – and didn't even look like numbers, look like Japanese or something.

EVELYN. What are you talking about? Same number it's always been.

CLIVE. *(a little loud)* Something different about it.

EVELYN. Shhh. Same number. And sit down, will ya?

(CLIVE sits down. He puts the bag on the table; it makes a thud – which EVELYN notices.)

CLIVE. Something different about it.

EVELYN. What you got in the bag, Clive?

CLIVE. Cause if it wasn't for the two trees – you know cause I recognize those – if it wasn't for them, I woulda said: that is not my house.

EVELYN. Well, it's a different color since last you been here.

CLIVE. *(pause, as this registers)* That's what it is! That's what it is. Cause my house was green – and black numbers – that was my house. And now it – what is it now?

EVELYN. It's blue, now – house is blue.

CLIVE. And red numbers. Why she do red? Black is the way you do a number. That's why I got confused.

EVELYN. Clive.

CLIVE. That's why I got confused.

EVELYN. What's in the bag, Clive?

CLIVE. *(a sigh of general confusion)* I don't know.

EVELYN. You don't know what you got in the bag?

CLIVE. I'm saying – I don't know about all a this. Cause this – this a very disordinary situation.

EVELYN. Let me see what you got in the bag.

(**CLIVE** *picks up the bag.*)

CLIVE. Why she paint the house blue? You like it that color?

EVELYN. Don't make no difference to me. *(pause)* Did you find me what I was looking for?

CLIVE. *(holding the bag)* Blue. Why she go with blue?

EVELYN. Let me see it.

CLIVE. Cause I don't like that color.

EVELYN. Clive – let me see what you got there.

(**EVELYN** *reaches across the table, attempting to take the bag from* **CLIVE** *– but he pulls it away from her.*)

CLIVE. Hey, now – don't be grabbing at that.

EVELYN. Just let me see what you got.

CLIVE. Grabbing like that! We gonna take this slow – cause, like I said, this a very disordinary situation.

EVELYN. I'm sorry.

CLIVE. Cause everything always moving too fast. But then sometimes you get it to move slow. And it go real slow, nice and easy – and then you see what you didn't see before.

(**CLIVE** *begins to untie the gold cord on the sack.*)

CLIVE. And everything go nice and easy. You see what I'm saying?

EVELYN. Nice and easy.

CLIVE. Alright, then.

(**CLIVE** *removes a small gun from the sack. Pause.* **EVELYN** *slowly, gently, holds out her hand.*)

EVELYN. Nice and easy.

(CLIVE hesitates.)

CLIVE. I don't know I'm gonna give it to you – so just hold on.

EVELYN. Give it to me.

CLIVE. Why we doing this? I don't remember. I don't understand why we doing this.

EVELYN. Just think of it like any deal you do.

CLIVE. But why you want this? I don't understand.

(EVELYN suddenly stands, goes over to the cupboard.)

EVELYN. You don't understand? Huh?

(EVELYN roots around in the back of the cupboard, pulls out an envelope.)

CLIVE. What you got there?

(EVELYN returns to table, sits. She pulls a pile of cash from the envelope, holds it up before CLIVE.)

EVELYN. Do you understand this?

(Pause; CLIVE regards the money.)

CLIVE. How much is that?

EVELYN. What we set: five hundred.

CLIVE. *(under the money's spell)* Five hundred dollar?

EVELYN. Yes.

CLIVE. How you have all that?

EVELYN. I work, Clive. I saved it.

CLIVE. A person can't save five hundred dollars. You don't make that much where you working. How much you make?

EVELYN. Been saving it for a long time. Since James was a baby. Was gonna be for his education.

CLIVE. Don't tell me that.

EVELYN. You asked me. But don't let that bother you. *(flashes money)* Just look at that, Clive. I bet that looks good to you.

CLIVE. *(indicating gun)* But why you want this? That's what I don't understand.

EVELYN. Is that how you conduct your business, Clive? That what you do when somebody wanna buy your other shit – you say, why you want that? Huh? Why you wanna buy this? You know, cause this ain't good for you – is that what you say?

CLIVE. This is not that.

EVELYN. Same thing, Clive – you need something, I need something. *(pause)* Five hundred dollars, Clive.

(pause)

CLIVE. Let me see. Count it out.

EVELYN. Let me first explain a little more about this transaction.

(pause)

CLIVE. I'm listening.

EVELYN. *(calmly)* You will give me that gun Clive –

CLIVE. *(interrupting)* Maybe I will give you this gun.

EVELYN. *(calm and confident)* No: you *will* give me the gun, Clive. Because I have a great deal of money in my hand. And you cannot resist that.

CLIVE. Don't tell me what I can or cannot do.

EVELYN. Don't get offended, Clive. We're just talking a man's nature, here. So: you will give me that gun –

CLIVE. Don't keep saying that!

EVELYN. Shhh. And I will give you this money – all of it.

CLIVE. Cause if I take it – it's only because I got things I could do with that money. Cause I got plans.

EVELYN. I'm sure you do. But the thing is, Clive – don't look at the money, look at me – if I give it to you, there a certain promise you have to make me.

CLIVE. What's that?

EVELYN. Cause don't think I'm giving you all this money for that little gun.

CLIVE. *(defensive)* It's worth it though – this a good gun – ain't nothing wrong with this gun.

EVELYN. Happy to hear that – but: this money is for something else, too.

CLIVE. *(impatient)* What else it for? You know you just like her – you drag everything out. What? What else it for?

EVELYN. If I give this to you, I don't ever want to see you in this house again – ever. You have to promise me that you will never show your face in this house again.

CLIVE. You can't tell me that.

EVELYN. Yes – I can.

CLIVE. This not just your house – it my house too.

EVELYN. No. Used to be your house. Remember – your house was green. But this blue house, that's my house. When my son died because of people like you – sick, disgusting people like you – then this stopped being your house.

(pause)

CLIVE. *(injured)* I see. That how you feel, huh? *(pause)* Just count out the money, then. Because I was going away anyway.

(EVELYN slides the money across the table toward CLIVE.)

EVELYN. Count it yourself.

(CLIVE puts the gun on his lap, and begins to count the money.)

EVELYN. What? You think I'm trying to cheat you? It's all there.

CLIVE. Always count. Always gotta count.

(CLIVE continues to count the money.)

CLIVE. Five hundred.

EVELYN. Now give me mine.

CLIVE. Well, we'll have to see about that, Evie. Sick, disgusting person like me don't always keep their promises.

(CLIVE takes the gun from his lap, stands.)

CLIVE. Besides, I don't know you can handle this.

(EVELYN pursues CLIVE.)

EVELYN. Don't you dare – give me that! Give it to me!

CLIVE. Now *you* gonna wake her up.

EVELYN. Give it to me. Give it to me or I will –

CLIVE. What? What you gonna do?

(pause; a standoff)

EVELYN. If you a man of your word, Clive – then you will give me that gun.

(pause)

EVELYN. Are you a man of your word, Clive? Cause if you ain't that, you're nothing.

(pause)

CLIVE. Well, I guess you can't shoot me – cause it not loaded. So: here you go, sister – you get the prize. You get the prize.

(He hands over gun to EVELYN. She clutches it desperately, backs away from CLIVE.)

EVELYN. *(trembling)* You know, Clive: it don't matter if there's no bullets in it now Matters if there's bullets in it if you ever try to come back in this house again. That's when you should be concerned if that gun loaded or not.

CLIVE. Why's that? *(laughs)* You gonna shoot me?

EVELYN. That's the whole point, Clive – cause I am telling you, if you ever come back here again, I will use this on you. And don't think I won't.

(pause)

CLIVE. You hate me that much, Evie?

EVELYN. *(pause)* I would turn that gun on you, as easy as I would on my– …I wouldn't hesitate, Clive.

CLIVE. Easy as what? On yourself, right? Maybe you wanna use it on yourself. Don't think I didn't think about that.

EVELYN. Well, that is a possibility, Clive. Thank you for mentioning that. So, let me see, you thought about that – but you still decided to give me the gun.

CLIVE. *(pause, flustered)* You know, because I, I – no, I didn't, I'm not saying –

EVELYN. Don't need to explain yourself. Cause that is certainly a possibility. That is not a thought unfamiliar to me. *(pause)* But – if I happen to still be around, and you try to come back here – I will be just as happy to use it on you.

(pause)

CLIVE. This who we are, huh? This here – this us, huh?

EVELYN. Yes. This who we are now. This who we gonna be.

(pause)

(**EVELYN** *sits at the table, holding the gun in her lap; she drifts away.*)

(**CLIVE** *looks at the money.*)

CLIVE. That fine with me, you know. Cause I got plans. I got it all mapped out. Cause I was going anyway.

EVELYN. So you said.

CLIVE. So don't think you got control over me.

EVELYN. *(indicating gun)* All I have is this.

(pause)

CLIVE. California. That, that's what we thinking about – you know, cause Ross thinking a coming with me.

(This gets **EVELYN** *'s attention.)*

EVELYN. I didn't know you see him anymore.

CLIVE. Now and then. Lately we been hooking up. Cause, you know, that who I got the gun from.

EVELYN. This – this is Ross's gun?

CLIVE. Was.

(**EVELYN** *laughs – darkly.*)

CLIVE. What?

EVELYN. It's just perfect, that's all. It's just beautiful. That this should be his gun. Life is so perfect, Clive – don't you think? So perfect, the way everything fall into place.

CLIVE. I guess. I don't know.

(**CLIVE** *has begun to count the money again.*)

EVELYN. You didn't tell him who the gun was for, did you?

CLIVE. Who?

EVELYN. Ross.

CLIVE. *(still counting money)* I didn't tell him nothing. My deal. *(He finishes counting.)* Why? You still got something for him?

EVELYN. I never had anything for him.

CLIVE. Did once.

EVELYN. Long time ago. And that was hardly nothing. I don't give him any thought.

CLIVE. *(defending his friend)* Well, he don't think on you either – never even ask about you.

EVELYN. As it should be. Like I said, perfect. Perfect world we living in.

(*Long pause.* **CLIVE** *keeps glancing at his money.*)

CLIVE. I guess I should tell her I'm going.

EVELYN. No – don't be waking her up.

CLIVE. She would want me to.

EVELYN. You wake her up, Clive – you never gonna get outta here. What – you want her grabbing at you – trying to get you to stay? You wanna be free, Clive – and she just gonna hold you back.

CLIVE. Yeah, she do grab on.

EVELYN. Make me sick the way she hangs on you.

CLIVE. I should say something to her, though – I made a promise on her today. Cause that would be wrong to just walk out like that.

EVELYN. *(gently, but deadly)* No, wouldn't be wrong. Best way is to just walk out. Way you always done it. *(pause)* I'll tell her goodbye for you.

(CLIVE is uncertain.)

EVELYN. And this ain't to do with her, anyway.

CLIVE. Alright, then. *(pause)* Tell her about my plans. That I got it all mapped out. Tell her she don't gotta worry about me.

EVELYN. I will. *(pause)* Don't let me keep you.

(pause)

EVELYN. What?

CLIVE. I was just thinking how I go – you know – do I just walk out the door now?

EVELYN. That's how it's done, Clive. Just walk out the door.

(pause)

CLIVE. This not what I thought.

EVELYN. Never is what you thought.

CLIVE. What we were, Evie – that was alright. Before everything. What we were.

(pause)

EVELYN. No getting back there. *(pause)* See now, how it's done: you open the door.

(CLIVE stands by the door, does not open it.)

EVELYN. You open the door.

(CLIVE opens the door.)

EVELYN. And after you walk out, you slam it real hard – so you know for sure that door closed.

CLIVE. I don't know who you are.

EVELYN. Slam it hard.

CLIVE. *(indicating money)* If I didn't have this…

EVELYN. Real hard, Clive – so there's no mistake.

(*CLIVE and EVELYN regard each other for a moment, then CLIVE leaves; he does not shut the door behind him.*)

(*pause*)

(*EVELYN gets up, goes over to the door, slams it hard – the sound is very loud, perhaps amplified.*)

(*pause*)

MAE'S VOICE. Clive? (*pause*) That you, Clive?

(*EVELYN returns to the table, puts the gun back in the sack.*)

MAE'S VOICE. Who out there? (*pause*) Clive?

EVELYN. It's just me.

MAE'S VOICE. What was that noise?

EVELYN. Nothing, Mama. Go back to sleep.

(*EVELYN sits down, the sack in her lap.*)

(*pause*)

(*MAE appears in the hallway.*)

MAE. I thought I heard something.

EVELYN. Nothing to hear.

(*Pause. MAE walks sleepily into the kitchen.*)

MAE. Boy, did I fall. I fell right out. (*pause*) What you still doing up?

EVELYN. Don't worry about me. Go back to bed.

MAE. Clive not back yet?

EVELYN. No.

MAE. I thought I heard him.

EVELYN. No.

MAE. Oh, I was having such dreams. He was inside one a those – that probably why.

EVELYN. In your mind – that's all.

MAE. Inside a dream. *(pause)* He was telling me something and I was laughing. Remember how he use to tell those funny stories? I don't remember the story, but in the dream I was laughing. Could you hear me laughing out here?

EVELYN. No.

MAE. *(touching her head)* Oh, I hope I not gonna have a headache tomorrow. Cause we got a lot to do tomorrow.

EVELYN. Better get to bed then.

MAE. You too, girl. Don't bother waiting up for him. You know him. He gonna be late. *(pause)* Oh, you know who else was in my dream? – Shorty Ross.

EVELYN. Oh, yeah?

MAE. He was dancing in that dream. He was a good dancer, that one.

EVELYN. That he was.

(pause)

MAE. I wasn't gonna tell you, but – he was here today – with your brother.

EVELYN. And you let him in the house?

MAE. He was already here when I got home. And don't be like that. He asked on you.

EVELYN. I don't think so.

MAE. Yes. All about you. Evelyn this and Evelyn that. I thought maybe we have him over to dinner sometime.

EVELYN. That man is not welcome here, Mama – and you know that.

MAE. Never gave you a hard time.

EVELYN. Never gave me nothing, Mama.

MAE. He gave you your boy – gave you Jame James.

(pause)

EVELYN. Yes, he did. And then that was the end of it.

(pause)

MAE. I know you get lonely.

(**MAE** *comes up behind* **EVELYN**, *puts her hands on her daughter's shoulders –* **EVELYN** *tries to shrug her off.*)

MAE. Stop now – I'm not gonna – I'm just touching you.

(**EVELYN** *allows* **MAE** *to touch her. Pause.*)

EVELYN. *(quiet, but insistent)* We don't need anybody else in our house. We don't, Mama.

MAE. Alright. Just the three of us then – you and me and your brother.

EVELYN. And if he goes away – the two of us.

MAE. He's not going anywhere – cause we gonna make it so he wanna be here.

(*Pause;* **MAE** *is still touching* **EVELYN**'s *shoulders – gently rocking her.*)

EVELYN. You go on to bed. I'll wait up for him.

MAE. What you got there?

EVELYN. What?

MAE. In the bag.

EVELYN. Just some old junk I was looking through.

MAE. You don't have to wait up for him.

EVELYN. I'm not tired.

MAE. Close your eyes.

EVELYN. Why?

MAE. Gonna get you to sleep.

EVELYN. How you gonna do that?

MAE. Close your eyes. *(pause)* Are they closed?

EVELYN. Yes.

(**EVELYN**, *in fact, does not close her eyes.* **MAE** *continues to rock her.* **EVELYN** *holds the sack to her breast.*)

MAE. Just keep them closed. And listen to your Mama.

(*pause*)

EVELYN. What?

MAE. Shhh. Listen to your Mama.

(MAE begins to sing: the song is a lullaby.)

MAE.
>All the children must sleep
>All the children are sleeping
>For it's night and there's nothing
>But singing or weeping
>
>All the children must sleep
>All the children are sleeping
>For to grow in their strength
>Soon there's singing and weeping
>
>All the children must sleep
>All the children are sleeping
>This song from the mother
>God charged with your keeping
>
>This song from the mother
>God charged with your keeping.

(MAE – whose own eyes are fluttering toward sleep – continues to rock EVELYN. EVELYN's eyes remain wide open.)

EVELYN. *(softly, not turning to look at MAE)* Go to bed, Mama. Go to bed.

(Slowly the lights fade to black.)

End of Play

www.ingramcontent.com/pod-product-compliance
Lightning Source LLC
Chambersburg PA
CBHW070648300426
44111CB00013B/2330